REALS

of

LIFE

REALS

of

LIFE

50 Real-Life Stories of Faith

MICHELLE HARGUS

DRY BONES PUBLISHING

For information about special discounts for bulk
purchases or author interviews, appearances, and
speaking engagements please contact:

DryBonesRanchNC@gmail.com

First Edition

ISBN hardcover: 979-8-9912747-0-8
ISBN softcover (color): 979-8-9912747-1-5
ISBN softcover (b&w):   979-8-9912747-3-9
ISBN ebook: 979-8-9912747-2-2

Library of Congress: 2024919310

Edited, book, and cover design by Rodney Miles
www.RodneyMiles.com
Images © Michelle Hargus

"Write everything I tell you in a book."

<u>Jeremiah 30:2</u>

There's a story behind the picture on the cover. A story about learning to trust.

Our son was living in Utah at the time. My husband and I were visiting him. Some friends invited us to go on a ride to check on some colts. We were able to ride horseback into the beautiful mountains of Utah to check on some yearlings. While that's not our son on the cover, a friend of his roped that filly because of a huge gash in her back leg. We weren't trying to hurt her at all. We only wanted to help her. However, she was scared and of course she didn't trust any of us.

Well, I realized while making this book, the whole book is really about trust. Trusting my heavenly Father. As my first book, I didn't have a clue what I was doing. However, I believe I would have been doing Him a disservice if I didn't at least try. I believe trusting Him through the entire process has led me to where we are today... Finished.

And that's pretty dang cool to me.

CONTENTS

PREFACE

WHEN I THINK back to where this may have all began, I remember telling my kids I wanted a Facebook page. They both told me I didn't need one, that I didn't have time for one. However, I have been known throughout my life not to be the best listener. Maybe even a tiny bit hard-headed. In this case, I'm kinda happy I went against what they both suggested. Because... I don't know if this adventure would have ever come full circle had I not gotten one.

I found myself posting stories, real-life things that were happening in and all around our family. Things that I felt like God was helping me pen down in my notes on my phone. Sometimes I couldn't quit thinking about what He helped me write so I would post my thoughts on Facebook. Then I would have peace and move on with the rest of my day.

People who read these stories seemed to relate to them. Some of my friends began telling me, "That story was just for me." Others started encouraging me to write a book. For years, so much enthusiasm and so many people encouraging me helped me believe that somebody who was not already my friend on FB may truly want to read what was written.

At first I called these things "inserts." Now they are considered "chapters." It took me a long time before I called these compiled "chapters" a REAL BOOK. The hardest part seems to be, for me, saying out loud that it's "mine," and that I actually wrote it. I can hardly see to type for the tears... for the years that this compilation represents. Overwhelming gratitude is all I know to call what I'm experiencing. It is so surreal to think this truly has come to fruition.

I can't take responsibility for these words without crediting my Heavenly Father for sitting with me while each story came to mind. Many of them started developing in the stillness of the night and/or early mornings when I would be spending time with Him.

My prayer is that as you read these words you will be blessed, and know that He is God. And that Jesus is real. And that He wants you to spend time with Him as well.

Thank You, Father!

I hope you enjoy this book. This REAL BOOK. My book. From the bottom of my heart... Thank You!

Michelle Hargus
Granite Falls, North Carolina
August, 2024

ADVENTURES OF LIFE

EVERYONE HAS A story. Everyone! Some people may think they know your story. However, nobody knows every chapter or each detail. God knows every particular there is to know. He cares about every aspect of our lives no matter how minute we think they may seem. There are different pages, seasons, or adventures, as I like to call them. Each experience we go through either brings us closer to God... or takes us further from Him. It's up to us. It's our choice. Choice, thank goodness, is one of the many gifts He has given us.

As I look back on my life, God has never left me! He can't! His word says...

Deuteronomy 31:6

Be STRONG and of GOOD courage,
do not fear nor be afraid of them;
for the Lord your God,
He is the One who goes with you.
He will not leave you or forsake you.

That says to me, He has never left my side and He never will! "Be strong and of good courage..." that's a command, not a suggestion.

Oh, what the Lord has done for me! For us all, for that matter! I could go on and on and on about His part in EVERY situation in my life! I won't get into any details... just yet anyway. But I will say this... God is GOOD! And His mercy endures forever! He is worthy to be praised!

Blessings to you all!

<u>Psalm 136:2 NKJV</u>

Oh, give thanks to the Lord,
for He is good.
For His Mercy endures forever.

BECOMING AWARE

WHEN WE FIRST got married, things were very different than they are now. We talked to each other differently. Well, I yelled and he shut down. I competed for his attention which had an opposite effect. I thought the way to communicate was to hash it out. Or fight. That's how I grew up. We both did. But our mechanisms were very different.

I remember staying at my aunt's house when I was little, thinking... *Oh man, they're probably gonna get a divorce because they don't scream and fight!* That was what I thought anyway. Pretty messed up, huh? It's like we had a force against us at all times. Later, we realized, we did!

The enemy hates marriage! He will try to do whatever he can to steal our peace. He sure tried with us! Actually, we let him succeed more times than I want to admit. However, it doesn't have to be that way! We allowed jealousy to almost destroy us. We let insecurities that we both carried tear us apart instead of grow us closer together. Which is what we both wanted. Those insecurities became a force that we had to learn to fight. We had to learn *not* to fight each other. We had to learn to fight the enemy instead.

Kevin, my husband, says I was "moldable." He thinks he has "trained" me. LOL! He may be right. I'll be the first to admit, he had and still has his work cut out for him. Well... I am so thankful we both allowed God to intervene. We began to learn how and tried our best to put Him first in everything. If we had not, we wouldn't be here today. Trust me... it wasn't easy. To this day, we still have to bite our tongues, and...

Let. It. Go!

I think all y'all young'uns need to hear this stuff. Actually, I know, no matter what age you are, we ALL need to have this strategy in our arsenal of weapons against the enemy.

One of the biggest things for me was just getting in the truck and going with him. Wherever! His hobbies have evolved over the years. And mine have revolved around him. I was even jealous of his hobbies! I thought he should stay home with me and the kids and "help me." So,

I would stay home and be miserable and that in turn would make him miserable while he was gone AND when he returned. Whew! Glad that's over!

Anyway... I hope this helps someone sooner than later especially before it's too late. Here's a nugget... Resist the enemy and he will flee. To put it another way... just bite your tongue and Let. It. Go.

Just some things to think about.

Isaiah 43:18 NIV

Forget the former things,
do not dwell on the past.

{ 3 }

TRUST

I THINK IT'S safe to say, we have all needed rescuing at some point in our lives. I was talking to a gal at a grocery store recently when she said to me, "I really struggle with trusting God." When she said that, I cringed inside and out. Not a scared cringe, just a cringe knowing what it may take to develop trust for our Heavenly Father. I've thought about it... trust is something that doesn't always come easy.

As we learn to trust God, it's usually during the times we have needed rescuing. God has rescued me so many times. Every time actually. This made me ponder some of the times in my life that seemed extremely challenging. We have all had them. The things no one knows about. The nights I begged for Him to rescue me from one thing or another. The nights I begged Him to rescue someone I love. Times when I've cried out to Him to rescue people I've never met! Some people honestly think they know what a person has been through, when they actually have no clue at all. What's said about "You can't understand someone until you've walked a mile in their shoes" is so very true.

When I think back on what I thought were rough spots in my life, I'm actually thankful for them all! So very thankful for each one BECAUSE during those not so easy seasons, that's when the trust for my Father started to grow. That's when I started to learn how to really trust Him. That's why I'm thankful for the tough spots and the long nights. I was just in His training and didn't even realize it.

"It always works out." That's been a motto of mine for years. That kind of goes along with, "This too shall pass." Which—guess what—is NOT actually in God's word. But we say it in hopes that this too shall pass. And if we believe... God will! He ALWAYS does... when we trust our Father. Jesus actually has already rescued us from anything and everything we could ever experience when He died for us on that cross. Yep. It's already done. TETELESTAI[1]! IT IS

---

[1] The Greek word "τετέλεσται" (tetelestai) is used in the Gospel of John as Jesus' last words ("it is finished") before He gave up His spirit on the cross. "Tetelestai" comes from the Greek root

FINISHED! Don't get me wrong... it may not be the way we think or want but He ALWAYS comes through. And it's always a better way than we could ever have imagined.

Have you ever forged a weapon? Well, I imagine it's a daunting task. Yep, the enemy sees us SO valuable that he forms weapons against us constantly. However, if we are God's and we TRUST Him and BELIEVE His word... guess what? No weapon formed against us shall prosper! We are SO valuable to our Father. The enemy couldn't care less about us. He's already been defeated and wants us to fail as well. The last thing he wants is for us to learn to TRUST God!

Hear this... Trust in His word today and believe that those long night cries will leave in Jesus name. But while you are there, learn to cherish those moments with Him and steep in His love. He WILL rescue you. He always does. He already has. Trust Him. Thank You Jesus!

---

word of "telew" meaning to bring to an end, finish, or complete.
—https://voxchurch.org/page/688?Item=486

<u>2 Corinthians 4:17-18 NKJV</u>

For our light affliction, which is but for a
moment, is working for us a far more
exceeding and eternal weight of glory, while
we do not look at the things which are seen,
but at the things which are not seen.
For the things which are seen are temporary,
but the things which are not seen are eternal.

REFLECTION

I WAS LOOKING in a lighted magnifying mirror in a department store. I probably need to get one. However, when I began focusing on my face, I saw things I had not seen before. Flaws, that with just my regular eyes, I don't normally see. As I continued to stare at them, I felt myself becoming discouraged at all the imperfections. Some, maybe, from what we call "growing older," or probably other imperfections that have always been there, that I just don't normally see.

Later during the week, I kept thinking about that face. My face. In the reflection I saw a mouth that spits out things that it just shouldn't say. I saw eyes that have seen things I wish they had never seen, which made me think about my mind, which is where our biggest battles take place.

When we focus on the negative, we can't help but see the negative. We then think about all the flaws. I'm thankful my Father doesn't look at me through a magnifying glass. When He looks at me, because of Jesus and what He has done for us all... He doesn't see me or my imperfections. He just sees Jesus. When He looks at me, I look perfect to Him. If you believe in Jesus, and have a relationship with Him, then the same goes for you as well my friend. Wow. Thank You Jesus! Thank You Father for Your Son!

Just something to think about. I don't think I'll buy that mirror either. LOL. Have a great day!

Jesus is not a window showing us who we can become, He is a mirror showing us who we already are.

—Unknown

<u>John 3:16 NKJV</u>

For God so loved the world that He gave His only begotten Son, that whoever believes in Him should not perish but have everlasting life.

{ 5 }

SO THANKFUL

ONE OF MY most favorite gifts my husband could ever give me... is the fact that he loves God the way he does. Most mornings, he is up before me, sitting in his spot, visiting with Him. What a gift. What a blessing. It wasn't always this way. Trust me, we have had our seasons of definitely not putting God first. But I prayed. Boy did I pray.

I remember a time when I stood in the very kitchen he has his quiet time in with God. I raised my hands to Heaven and said, "Here he is Lord! I've tried to change him. I can't do it. But You sure can. It's not my responsibility, anyway. So here he is! I'm giving him back to you!"

From that moment on, I began trusting and thanking God for the man he would become. And *He* did! What I mean is, my Heavenly Father did it! Wives and/or husbands, if you want this for

15

yourself, then let me tell you a secret. You sure can't "gripe" him or her into a relationship with Christ. Be sneaky about it! Pray him/her into it! And thank God for it even before you see it happening. Yep.

We have authority over the enemy and I suggest if this is something you desire of your husband or your wife, or someone you love, go to WAR! And fight for them! Trust God. Love your husband well. And get excited! You may be the only thing standing between his relationship with our Creator. Ouch. Just something to think about.

Proverbs 27:15-16 MSG

A nagging spouse is like the drip, drip, drip
of a leaky faucet...
you can't turn it off, and you can't get
away from it..

6

TENDER WHISPER

THE TENDER WHISPER of love in the dead of night... have you heard it? When I hear people being mad about being woken up and not being able to go back to sleep, I remember doing the same thing.

I learned many years ago when this happens, not to be angry about it... but to spend time with my Father instead. Whether you get out of bed or not, don't be frustrated or you may miss Him. See it as an opportunity. My go-to place is in our basement. I find so much peace there. Make it a habit and you will learn to look forward to those minor sleep interruptions. So rejoice and be thankful for the quietness of the night. Do it your way. However that looks. Just spend time with your Father. You can read, pray, listen, or just be quiet and still your mind. You may even cry really long and really hard. Whatever you do, just do it. And don't miss it.

Some of my most precious visits with Him have been in the dead of night. That may be the only time He can get our attention. Our days can be long, loud, busy, and chaotic. He doesn't like to compete with that. He will if He has to, but it may be more unpleasant than losing a little sleep.

Next time you can't sleep, even if it was because of that pizza, don't grumble, just talk to your Father. Spend time with Him. And love every minute of it. He wants us to visit with Him.

That tender whisper of love in the dead of night. What a beautiful thing. He is so amazing!!

Now go have an awesome day!

<u>Proverbs 8:17 KJV</u>

I love them that love Me;
and those that seek Me early
shall find Me.

7

KNOW HIS PROMISES

"IT IS FINISHED!" it was a roar... a lion's roar! Jesus said... "TETELESTAI!" His last words on the cross. Thank you, Jesus!

Overflow with confidence in His promises.

Romans 15:13 Amplified Bible

May the God of all hope fill you with all joy and peace in believing (through the experience of your faith) that by the power of the Holy Spirit you will abound in hope and overflow with confidence in His promises!

Woo-hoo! Now that's something to get excited about. Here's a nugget... there is a promise in God's Word for every situation you may be experiencing or will ever go through. If you do not know the promises He has for you, now is the time to search them out! As long as you have breath or your loved one has breath, there is still hope and it's not too late!

Go to God's Word and find your promises! Google them if you want! Write them down! Make a commitment today to stand on them! Write them on a piece of paper and put them in your shoe if you have to! You can do that too! But what I'm really trying to say is... write them on your heart and most of all... BELIEVE THEM!

Then tell the enemy what God has promised you! Resist the enemy and he will flee! He has to! Because that's a promise as well! But if you don't know, you don't know! So go know! Put forth an effort on your part! Take one step, trust and believe, and God will light your way. He will even make your crooked paths straight. That's a promise, too, if you believe Him.

Yes, IT IS FINISHED! However, we need to stand on His promises instead of dwelling on our problems. And when you "overflow with confidence in His promises," some people won't understand. Do it anyway!!!

Something to think about.

<u>2 Corinthians 1:20 NKJV</u>

For all the promises of God in Him are Yes, and in Him Amen, to the glory of God through us.

{ 8 }

KNOWLEDGE IS POWERFUL

LET'S SAY WE are all soldiers and each one of us is at war. We all have access to the same weapons. They were issued to us at the beginning of time. However, only a very few actually know what or how to use these weapons. Most have no idea how to fight in a battle. Most of us don't even realize we have any weapons at all. So we perish. Our loved ones perish. For lack of knowledge. What if children's lives would be spared if parents knew they had these weapons for warfare?

I was just now asleep and woke up suddenly thinking about a phone call I received today. As I lay in bed, I started listing names of friends who I know recently have lost different battles. Battles that I believe were spiritual. I could fill a sheet of paper quickly with many names. I also believe every battle is spiritual and that everything we face is spiritual.

When my thoughts race like that, I might as well get out of bed and write them down, otherwise I usually won't rest again until I do.

Driving a week or so ago I was praying for someone who I pray for quite often, when all of a sudden a strong feeling of strength came over me. A spiritual strength, I believe. Something like a surge of confidence in what I was praying for. A breakthrough possibly. You see, I was accessing my arsenal for weapons. When all of a sudden a hawk swooped down and soared right in front of me. Not close enough for me to hit it, but close enough for me to see his strength. It was like time stood still for a second. This may sound freaky, but for me...

It. Was. Very. Powerful.

I've had incidents with hawks before... and I believe that hawk was there for a purpose. It was not a coincidence. I found this a while ago. The hawk symbolizes the ability to use intuition and higher vision in order to complete tasks or make important decisions.

Animal guides can deliver important messages to us from beyond, and hawks definitely serve as animals that can heighten our spiritual awareness and helps us along our paths. I believe that God sent that hawk for me to see as reassurance that what I was praying... was in motion. Thank you, Father!

This may all sound weird but think about this... God says, "My people are destroyed (perish) for lack of knowledge." So who's at fault? If you are reading this... it's not a coincidence either. Maybe God woke me up so He could help me write this down for someone He's been trying to get the attention of. Why not? Maybe He's trying to help you know these things to prepare you for the battle ahead? Or the battle you are facing now? And the only way you or your loved one has a chance, is if you know about His weapons in that book He's given us... His Word.

SO thankful that we are learning about these weapons of warfare! As I think back about SO many things we've walked through... I couldn't imagine not having them in our arsenal.

Just something to think about.

<u>2 Corinthians 10:4</u>

The weapons we fight with are not the weapons of the world. On the contrary, they have divine power to demolish strongholds.

9

LEARNING TO LISTEN

WHEN YOU DON'T know what's going on... trust and obey. When you feel you're living a mystery... trust and obey. When you have no idea what you're doing, why people do the things they do, where your prodigal son or daughter is, whether a loved one will live or die... trust and obey. When you don't know what your next step in life will be ...

You get what I'm saying?

Through our lives, tough times will come. Learn to trust your Father. Trust Him. Tell him every detail. He wants us to. Then praise Him, thank Him, and listen for His voice. Then obey what He tells you. That takes effort on our part.

One thing I have learned... We have a part to play, a huge part. A functioning part.

1. Tell your Father every detail of your life. What's going on that you want to talk to Him about. He loves all the details.

2. Then praise Him for who He is.

3. Then thank Him.

4. Then TRUST Him for the answer or the result. All prayer is, is a conversation with your Father. You can constantly be in prayer with Him just by being thankful.

5. Learn to listen for His voice. Holy Spirit wants to comfort you, not bark commands.

When you become aware of His voice... you will hear Him more and more. When we trust Him and learn to listen... our heart, our gut, His word... It gets easier to hear Him the next time and the next and the next.

I jotted this down early one morning. I didn't know... but He knew I would need this later that day. He always knows. So I prayed. Then I remembered what I jotted down. Then I praised Him. Then I thanked him. Oh how I trust Him! Thank you Father! Thank you Jesus! Thank you Holy Spirit!

He loves us SO much.

<u>Proverbs 3:5-6 NKJV</u>

Trust in the Lord with all your heart, And
lean not on your own understanding; In all
your ways acknowledge Him,
and He shall direct your paths.

10

LOVE... NOT JUDGE

WHAT IF WE took a good look at ourselves, on the daily, instead of critiquing everyone around us constantly? What if we saw our own possibilities and positivities instead of what we don't like about ourselves? What if we asked ourselves, *How did God create us to be?* Not how we think we *should* be. What if we look at others' full potential rather than putting them down? What God has put inside of them, instead of the outward obvious? What if we told them what they are capable of, in a loving way, instead of how sorry we think they are being? What if we made an effort to consciously build people up instead of constantly tearing them down?

What if we saw others' good qualities instead of focusing on their not-so-good? What if we had negative thoughts enter our mind about the ones we love and we said, "NO!" then moved on to a positive about them, and dwelt on those thoughts instead? What if we actually told the ones we love good things they do instead of screaming all the wrong... every single day. If we critiqued ourselves instead of everyone else? If we practiced seeing the good in others instead of the negative? If we practiced seeing the good in ourselves instead of seeing what we think is wrong with us... every day. I believe things would change. I believe our minds would change. I believe our hearts would change. I believe freedom would come to our minds, and to the ones we love and the negatives would turn into positives.

Today, let's focus on us and not try to change the ones we supposedly love... no matter what things may look like. Just love them anyway. The way they are. Love others like our Father loves us. So thankful for His mercy!

I believe if we started speaking life into others, their lives would change. We would change. Things would be different. For the better.

"If you judge people,
you have no time to love them."

—Mother Teresa

Matthew 7:1-2 TPT

Refuse to be a critic full of bias toward
others, and you will not be judged.
For you'll be judged by the same standard
that you've used to judge others. The
measurement you use on them will be used
on you.

11

PRAYER OF PROTECTION

PSALM 91 HAS been a favorite prayer of mine many times over the years during different seasons and adventures of my life. Sometimes, I would pray Psalm 91 all through the night for someone and or over myself. I've walked our property and the property of others praying this very Psalm as a prayer. Psalm 91 is a prayer of protection you may want to pray today and keep close to your heart in days to come:

~

Father, I praise You that I dwell in the secret place of the Most High, and that I shall remain stable and fixed under the shadow of the Almighty [Whose power no foe can withstand]. I will say of You, Lord, "The Lord is my Refuge and my Fortress, my God; on Him I lean and rely, and in Him I confidently trust!"

For then You will deliver me from the snare of the fowler and from the deadly pestilence. Then You will cover me with Your pinions [feathers], and under Your wings shall I trust and find refuge. Your truth and Your faithfulness are a shield and a buckler.

I shall not be afraid of the terror of the night, nor the arrow [the evil plots and slanders of the wicked] that flies by day, nor of the pestilence that stalks in darkness, nor of the destruction and sudden death that surprise and lay waste at noonday.

A thousand may fall at my side, and ten thousand at my right hand, but it shall not come near me. Only a spectator shall I be [inaccessible in the secret place of the Most High] as I witness the reward of the wicked.

Because I have made You, Lord, my refuge, and the Most High my dwelling place, their shall no evil befall me, nor any plague or calamity come near my tent. For You will give Your angels especial charge over me, to accompany and defend and preserve me in all my ways of obedience and service. Your angels shall bear me up on their hands, lest I dash my foot against a stone.

I shall tread upon the lion and adder. The young lion and serpent shall I trample underfoot. Because I have set my love upon You, therefore You will deliver me. You will set me on high, because I know and understand Your Name.

I have a personal knowledge of Your mercy, love, and kindness. I trust and rely on You, knowing You will never forsake me, no never. I shall call upon You, and You will answer me. You will be with me in trouble. You will deliver me and honor me. With long life will You satisfy me and show me Your salvation!

—Taken from The Amplified Bible

So thankful for Psalm 91! Please steep in it now! Stay in it always! Love it for yourself and the ones you love! This is the Secret Place. Dwell in His Shadow and be protected!

<u>Psalm 91: 1-3 KJV</u>

He that dwelleth in the secret place of the most High shall abide under the shadow of the Almighty. I will say of the Lord, He is my refuge and my fortress: my God; in Him will I trust. Surely He shall deliver thee from the snare of the fowler, and from the noisome pestilence.

12

I LOVE YOU FATHER

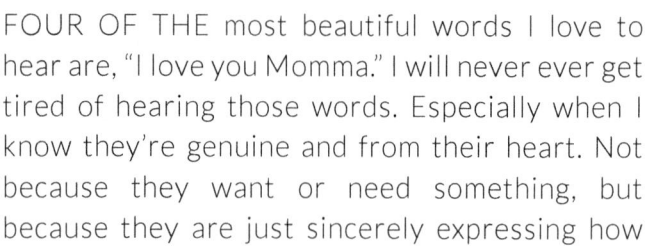

FOUR OF THE most beautiful words I love to hear are, "I love you Momma." I will never ever get tired of hearing those words. Especially when I know they're genuine and from their heart. Not because they want or need something, but because they are just sincerely expressing how they feel. Or what they know to be true.

I heard those words the other night and my eyes filled with tears and I melted just a bit. I was thinking about it later and I thought... *I bet our Father feels the same way.* So I just began to tell Him... *I love you Father!*

Just imagine Him smiling and getting all warm inside. Not because I wanted anything. I just truly wanted Him to know I love Him. Because I know HE loves me! If you haven't told Him in a while, tell Him! Say this... "I love you Father" or "I love you Jesus. I love you Holy Spirit" or "I love you Daddy. I love you Savior" or "I love You Father God. I love You Papa" or "I love you Friend!" Or all of the above! Whatever you call Him! Just tell Him!

That's a form of worship and praise. He doesn't really need us to do that... or does He? I think He wants us to! And I'm sure He likes it when we do! "I love you Momma."

One more thing... if you don't know that He loves you, well He does! Here's a reminder or how you may know...

John 3:16 NKJV

For God so loved the world, that He gave His only begotten Son, that whoever believes in Him will not perish but have everlasting life!

BELIEVE IN HIM!

<u>Isaiah 54:13 NKJV</u>

All your children shall be taught by the LORD, And great shall be the peace of your children.

13

NOTHING IS SECRET

A FRIEND GAVE me two verses several years ago. She said God told her to. However, she wasn't sure why those two. Five months later... God woke me up and I knew He was telling me to go read those two verses again. When I did, I knew at that very moment why these were given to me. Today I think we all need to know these two verses. We need to pray them. We need to believe them. Then we should watch with expectancy as they come to life. Remember His word is alive and active.

Pray these verses for our country. Pray these for justice to be revealed. However you stand, whatever you believe, whatever you're going through, the truth should be known in every situation, now and in our future. For the future of our children and our children's children.

<u>Luke 8:17 NKJV</u>

For nothing is secret that will not be revealed,
nor ANYTHING hidden that will not be
known and come to light.

<u>Matthew 10:26</u>

Therefore do not fear them. There is nothing
covered that will not be revealed, and hidden
that will not be known.

Some important things to think about.

Hebrews 4:12 ESV

For the word of God is living and active,
sharper than any two-edged sword, piercing
to the division of soul and of spirit, of joints
and of marrow, and discerning the thoughts
and intentions of the heart.

14

DO IT ANYWAY

THINK OF SOMETHING you want to do that you've never done. Stop. Think. Try. Got it? Now plan. Make an appointment. Write it on your calendar. Schedule it in your planner. Your phone. Your head. Now figure out how to make it happen. Otherwise, life happens and you will never do the things you want to do because there was no plan. Guilty!

If I wasn't married to Kevin, riding horses and horse stuff like roping probably wouldn't have been something I would have chosen. But I've always loved him. And we have pretty much always had and been around horses together since before we were married. So, if you can't beat'em, join'em, and then beat'em at their own game when possible. However, it doesn't come easy for me.

I'm awkward, a little goofy, and only sometimes determined. But I try. I have been trying 30 some years and would like to think I'm still trying. I'm probably not much better than I was then, but here I am, almost 55 and still trying to try.

Sometimes, nonetheless, I just don't want to—'cause I'm goofy, remember? I do some of the stupidest stuff. Even recently, one of our lifelong friends said to me, "Michelle, get over here. What is that stupid stuff you're doing in the box? That's the goofiest thing I've ever seen! Stop it!"

Thanks Kelly.

You've got to love honest friendships that speak truth into your life! Be thankful for them. Stuff like that is hard to hear but how do we get better if we don't listen?

My saddle is extremely heavy. The heaviest in the barn. My horse is tall. The tallest we own. Thankful Kevin usually saddles and I usually unsaddle 'cause I really struggle with that. But I go anyway.

Every time I ride, especially when I rope... I leak. Yep. I said it. Doesn't matter how many times I go before I get on the horse; I still go when on the horse. And if I forget the proper attire, then it's extremely noticeable. Like to my knees noticeable. And I don't care what you're thinking right now 'cause I'm just being honest.

That right there is enough to make me want to cry or be depressed and sad, enough that I could easily choose not to EVER swing my leg over a horse and rope again. But I don't choose that.

I say all of that to say this: *Live life large*. Do the scary things you don't want to do. Do them SCARED! Do them even if you do embarrassing things and people laugh at you, or you *think* they're laughing at you, (which they probably aren't). Just laugh with them! Heck, I laugh at myself so much, I leak then, too!

Lighten up. Do it scared. Leak a little! Or a lot! It's okay. Life is too short to sit at home wishing you would have done this or done that and be full of regrets. Just go do it! Whatever IT is! Be "blessed and unstoppable!" (Thanks for that quote, Billy Alsbrooks!)

If you know God, that's who we are! We are BLESSED AND UNSTOPPABLE! If you don't know Him... KNOW HIM! That's the Ultimate Adventure!

Thankful!

Something to think about.

<u>2 Timothy 1:7 NKJV</u>

For God has not given us a spirit of fear, but
of power and of love and of a sound mind.

15

PAY ATTENTION TO YOUR THOUGHTS

HOW WE THINK is SO important! We really need to pay attention to our thoughts. What's the first thing you think about when you wake up in the morning, even before you open your eyes?

I love when I wake up with a song playing in my head. Sometimes I'll even be singing it out loud as I'm waking up! I love it when that happens. Today, my very first thought was this... "When God sleeps, He dreams about me!" Yep. That was my first thought. And I believe it!

God's Word says He never slumbers or sleeps. I believe He thinks about us all the time. He loves us that much! You just need to KNOW it. Better yet, believe it. Think about it this way... Instead of dwelling on your problems or the issues the day

MAY hold, think about how much Your Father loves you. Dwell on that instead.

You may not believe it at first. But when you know, really KNOW that He loves you, your problems may seem to dissipate. When we focus on Him and His love for us, our problems don't look quite as big.

Just rest in His love today, precious one, and pay attention to your thoughts. He's thinking about us all the time! Let's think about Him.

Have a great day!

<u>Jeremiah 29:11 KJV</u>

For I know the plans I have for you, declares the Lord, plans to prosper you and not to harm you, plans to give you a hope and a future.

16

WHERE IS OUR GAZE?

DID YOU KNOW we have an opportunity—we have an opportunity to walk through fire? We all have difficulties at some point in our lives. But did you know we have an opportunity to walk through the fire of our circumstances and come out the other side without even the SMELL of smoke? Shadrach, Meshach, and Abednego showed us how to do it. Some of us have done it. Jesus was with them and He is with us. He walks through the fire with us as well.

Jesus tells us...

> "And surely I am with you always,
> to the very end of the age."
>
> —Matthew 28:20

Think about it like this... Where are our eyes looking? Where is our gaze? Are we looking down? Are we looking to the news, constantly? Are we staring at our phones, endlessly? What are we listening to? What are we reading? Instead of all of that stuff, we should be looking *up*. That's where our help comes from!

I'm not suggesting being ignorant to what's going on around us. I'm just stressing that our help comes from the Lord. He's already been here! He's here now. He's already taken anything and everything upon Himself that you or I could ever imagine, while He was ON that cross! Even the pain of a hangnail. EVERYTHING! All of what we could possibly experience in our life! Nothing is of any surprise to Him. Our part is to read His Word and know His promises. To believe and to trust Him. To trust Him with our everything!

We all have things in our lives that we have walked through that God has brought us out of. Remember what he's already done for our families and the people we read about in His Word. If you don't know what He's done, then go read about Him. If you don't know, you won't know! So go know! We all have a part to play in this game called life. Now let's play!

Guard your faith. If you don't have faith, GET YOU SOME! This is our heritage—faith, that is!

Did you know we are all given the same measure of faith? It's how we use it that determines if it grows... or not.

SAY THIS:

I lift up my eyes to the mountains—where does my help come? My help comes from the Lord, the Maker of heaven and earth.

Psalm 121:1-2 NIV

If He made Heaven and Earth... then I think we should trust Him, don't you?

Look up!

Something to think about.

<u>Psalm 121:1-2 NIV</u>

I lift up my eyes to the mountains-- where
does my help come? My help comes from the
Lord, the Maker of heaven and earth.

17

GOD OF RESTORATION

GOD SAID, "I'm restoring it as if it had never happened." God is the God of restoration. He reminded me of that a few days before Christmas. He WILL restore what the enemy TRIED to take away, from us and from the ones we love. But there is a part we have to play. I mean, I don't guess we HAVE to. But I think He WANTS us to. He wants us to KNOW that He is a God of restoration. To BELIEVE that. To TRUST Him to do that.

Then I saw this... "Call Me your Shepherd and I will carry you. Call Me your friend and I will listen to your heart's cry. Call Me your Redeemer and I will bring restoration to your soul." God's Word is ALIVE! His promises are YES! And AMEN! Which means *it is so*, or *I agree!*

I was reading in 2 Kings about a mother whose son was dead. Then he was brought back to life. A man named Elisha restored her son's life. Not only was the son's life restored, but seven years later the king ordered that all that was lost to the mother, and all the proceeds of the field from the day that she had left the land until now, that what the enemy tried to steal from her, would all be restored as well!

I say all that to say this, again... God is the God of restoration. He WILL restore what the enemy TRIED to take away. Trust Him. And BELIEVE Him! But once again, if you don't know, then you don't know. Read His Word. Know His promises.

At some point in your life, you will want to know how to stand. And in the deepest darkest of nights, you not only need to know how to stand, you need to know how to fight the enemy and how to fight him well. Then, to trust what you know to be right. Because if we don't prepare for war ahead of time... how will we know how to fight the enemy when he tries to attack? How will we know how to win?

Anyway, thank You Father for restoration!

Something to think about.

"There is nothing that is beyond God's power to MEND HEAL OR RESTORE."

—Christine Caine

<u>2 Kings 8:6</u>

And when the king asked the woman, she told him. So the king appointed an official for her, saying, "Restore all that was hers, together with all the produce of the fields from the day that she left the land until now."

18

MY NEEDS ARE MET

WHAT'S GOING ON in your head? Are you heavy? What's weighing you down? Well, sometimes we just get in a funk. Different things in our lives can cause us to look at our circumstances, and trust me... sometimes we just want to crawl back in bed, close our eyes and hope that it all goes away.

We all have stuff. We all have things. Disappointments. Pain in our bodies. People we love suffering through whatever their funk is at the time. Prodigals. Sicknesses. Storms of life, etc.

I'm not making light of any of it!

We live in a fallen world and we go through gunk. Here's the kicker: I messaged a friend one morning, who I had an appointment with, to cancel it 'cause I just didn't feel like going. I just wanted to stay in bed. This was his response:

"Just go ahead and give up and I'll see you whenever you are ready."

Hmmm, Give up? Was that what I was doing? Made me look at myself and come to the conclusion that sometimes when we are at our "heaviest," we just throw in the towel, not even realizing we are really just giving up. However, that's the worst thing we can do. We cannot give up! We just can't afford to!

What God showed me that morning was no matter what we're going through, my needs are met according to God's riches in glory through Christ Jesus! My needs are met!

Say this: "MY NEEDS ARE MET! In Jesus' name! Thank God!"

So whatever we are walking through… know this… Your needs have already been met! But we have to stand on that promise and most of all, BELIEVE it! Take your mind off your circumstances. Know this… You can't trust your "feelings" either. Get out of bed and especially, out of your head! Say out loud, "My needs are met!". My needs are met! Over and over until you believe it! And then all day, every day, thank Him for it! My needs are met! And so are yours. Have a great day!

<u>Philippians 4:19 NKJV</u>

And my God shall supply all your need according to His riches in glory by Christ Jesus.

19

EVERYTHING IS SPIRITUAL

CAN I SAY something? *Everything is spiritual.* Let me say that again. *EVERYTHING is spiritual!* The enemy hates you! He hates your family. He hates marriage. He hates the church. He works overtime to try to destroy your children, your life, your sanity. He does whatever it takes to destroy anything good.

That fight you just had with your husband... from the enemy. The things your kids go through... that's an attack. Division in your church? Chaos in your home? I'm telling you people, it's time we go to war and fight for what is ours. I'm so tired of the enemy trying to steal what doesn't belong to him.

He's a thief! The thief does not come except to steal, and to kill, and to destroy. Jesus came that we may have life, and that we might have it more abundantly. The next time the enemy tries to steal from you... FIGHT! We have to fight the right one. It's not your husband you need to fight, nor your family. It's not your children. Fight the right enemy instead! He's the real foe. And if the ones you love can't fight for themselves, then it's up to you to stand in the gap and fight for them!

I'm so mad at the enemy for trying to steal what does not belong to him. For we do not wrestle against flesh and blood, but against principalities, against powers, against spiritual hosts of wickedness in the heavenly places! *Everything is spiritual*... Think about it.

<u>Romans 12:2 NKJV</u>

And do not be conformed to this world, but be
transformed by the renewing of your mind,
that you may prove what is that good and
acceptable and perfect will of God.

20

THE GIFT OF CHOICE

IT'S HARD SOMETIMES. Life that is. And death. I know which one I like so far... up to this point anyway.

We found a steer down, sick and puny. His name was Pete. I named him after all the Pedialyte[2] I tried to give him. I wish I could tell y'all he was full of life and running to eat feed or hay, but I'm not. Once they go down, it's hard to get them back up. We've lost steers before. We've lost cows and calves before. But I've never tried so hard to save one. And as bad as it looked, we gave him every chance possible to help replenish his life. But nothing worked.

---

[2] Pedialyte® is scientifically formulated with the optimal balance of sugar and sodium electrolytes§ needed to help replenish fluids and electrolytes, the loss of which can lead to dehydration. —https://pedialyte.ca/en/what-is-pedialyte

Some might say, "He was just a steer." No, he was our responsibility to try everything possible, and I think we did. Kelly, one of our vets and precious friend, tried a last Hail Mary[3] with no improvement. We aren't farmers. We just like to rope. We don't raise cattle. We just own some roping steers and some momma cows. But we do care for them. And we sure did try with this one. I'm very sad Pete didn't make it. But I'm satisfied with what we did for him. I prayed the night before he died that if he wasn't gonna survive, he would just go on instead of us having to do it. And he did. Thank You, Father!

Death is inevitable for every living thing and every living person. Maybe Pete went to Heaven. I hope so. I don't know for sure. But what we do need to know for sure, each one of us, is that we choose Christ here, before we go there. There is Heaven... or hell. And here is where we make the choice.

Some things to think about.

---

[3] 1. : a Roman Catholic prayer to the Virgin Mary that consists of salutations and a plea for her intercession. 2. or less commonly Hail Mary pass : a long forward pass in football thrown into or near the end zone in a last-ditch attempt to score as time runs out. —https://www.merriam-webster.com/dictionary/Hail%20Mary

<u>Proverbs 12:10 NIV</u>

The righteous care for the needs of their animals, but the kindest acts of the wicked are cruel.

21

HE KNEW US BEFORE

I ASKED GOD not too long ago to remind me of when I asked Him into my heart. I couldn't remember when. I didn't have a "date." I just knew that I have always known Him. As far as I could remember, He has always been with me. I know I haven't always acted like it. And He knows all too well I sure made some stupid, wrong decisions in my life. But I still knew I KNEW Him. He's ALWAYS been with me. I just wanted to remember when we met this side of Heaven.

Well actually, God has ALWAYS known us. Before He created us, or sent us to Earth to live awhile, He knew us.

Anyway... I asked Him when. And He told me! He allowed me to remember when I was five, I was at a summer Bible School at the church we went to when I was little. They gave an invitation to know Him. I didn't hesitate. I went forward. I told a lady I wanted Jesus in my heart, and I wanted to fill out one of those little cards.

He reminded me of what happened next. She said, "Honey, go sit back down. You're too little to know what's going on. You just don't understand. You can do this when you're a little older."

OH NO SHE DIDN'T!

Yep. She did. BUT... that's okay! I believe with all my heart I knew Him at that church that very day! I asked Him into my heart at that church! I received Him in that pew all by myself! And I have known Him ever since.

That lady meant no harm. But I say that to say this... Be careful who you may turn away. Unknowingly and knowingly. God brings people across our paths on purpose. EVERY DAY! People who need God, who need us to help them! Certain ways we handle things may turn them to God or turn them away from God.

Integrity is what you do when no one is looking. Be careful how you help them... or don't help them. Be aware of your decisions on how you handle a job, on keeping your word... or not. Telling someone you'll do one thing... and not following through when they need you most. I'm not saying their salvation is on your shoulders...

Or is it?

Some things to think about for sure.

<u>Mark 10:13-16 NKJV</u>

Then they brought little children to Him,
that He might touch them; but the disciples
rebuked those who brought them. But when
Jesus saw it, He was greatly displeased and
said to them, "Let the little children come to
Me, and do not forbid them; for of such is the
kingdom of God. Assuredly, I say to you,
whoever does not receive the kingdom of God
as a little child will by no means enter it."
And He took them up in His arms, laid His
hands on them, and blessed them.

22

DRESS ACCORDINGLY

GOD'S ARMOR IS a game-changer. Our status as a child of God gives us rights and privileges others don't have. We are soldiers fully equipped! We need not fear anything, not even the enemy, Satan himself. God delivers us!

In Ephesians 6:14-17, God lays out His armor:

- **Belt of Truth**—to protect us against the enemy, the deceiver and liar.

- **Breastplate of Righteousness**—to represent our positional righteousness before God.

- **Shoes of the Gospel of Peace**—to ensure we are at peace with everyone and ready to go wherever God calls.

- **Shield of Faith**—to quench all of the enemy's fiery darts.

- **Helmet of Salvation**—to ensure we know we are a saved child of God, covered by Jesus' blood, possessing the mind of Christ.

- **Sword of the Spirit**—the Word of God and our only offensive weapon.

Satan has one primary weapon... Lies.

So, doesn't it make sense that we would only need one offensive weapon to wield against Him? That weapon is TRUTH. God's spirit dwells in each of us, and is able to do...

"… immeasurably more than all we ask or imagine, according to His power that is at work in us."

Ephesians 3:20

That power is…

"… far above all rule and authority, power and dominion, and every name that is invoked, not only in this present age but also in the one to come."

Ephesians 1:21

"… the one who is in you is greater than the one who is in the world."

1 John 4:4b

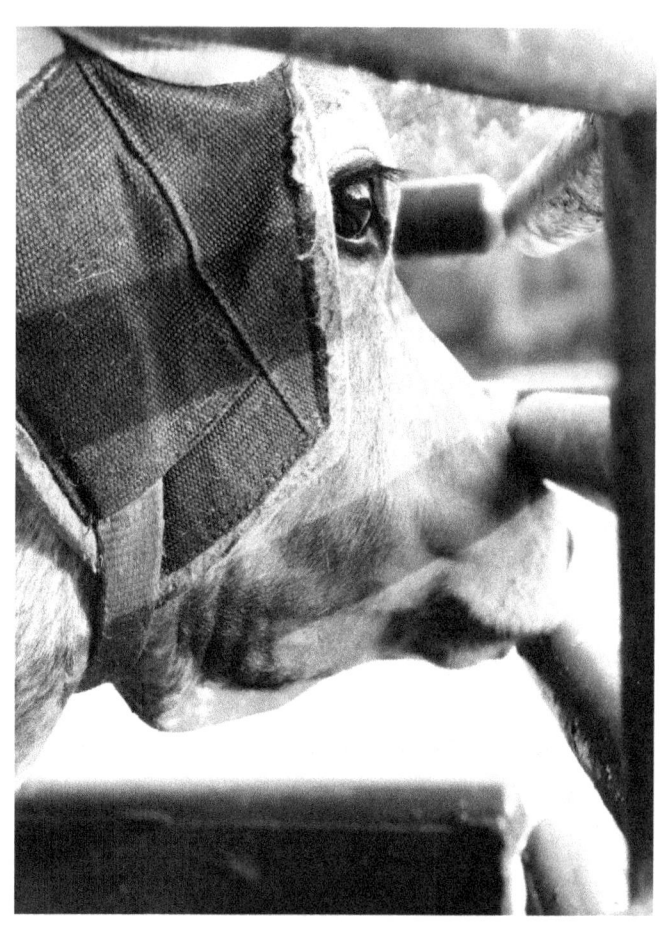

<u>Ephesians 6:13</u>

Therefore put on the full armor of God, so
that when the day of evil comes, you may be
able to stand your ground, and you have
done everything, to stand.

23

DON'T LET STRIFE IN

"STRIFE DROPS THE shield of faith, stops prayer results and invites Satan and his cohorts into your midst. Discord is deadly. It paralyzes the power of God in your life."[4]

Don't allow the enemy to stop you at your own front door by allowing strife in your home. If you do, you'll be no threat to him anywhere else.

Put the power of harmony to work in your family. In your workplace. In your church. Everywhere you go. Without our shield of faith... Hmmm, I don't even want to think about that. Yet

---

[4] From "Peace at Home" by Kenneth Copeland. — https://www.kcm.org/read/faith-to-faith/02/24?language_content_entity=en-US

we drop our shield, one of our most important weapons, when we don't walk in peace and trust.

Trust him.

Something to think about.

<u>Proverbs 20:3 TPT</u>

A person of honor will put an argument to rest. Only the stupid want to pick a fight.

24

WHAT A GOOD FRIDAY

GOOD FRIDAY WAS the worst day in history and the BEST day in history. Our church has an awesome service every Good Friday remembering what Christ did for us. One Good Friday in particular, I wore this beautiful white outfit with leggings and cute shoes. Anyway, I really hadn't thought about it being white... until we took communion. Communion or The Lord's Supper is, to me, a celebration of what He did for each of us where you take bread (in remembrance of Christ's body) and wine (in remembrance of Christ's blood). At the time, we drank grape juice at our church (as with any other church I've been to). Purple grape juice. At our church, we all walk down to the front while music is playing and get our communion elements.

My whole day had already been AWESOME. I had done some things I felt like I was supposed to do. Things I felt like in my heart, God TOLD me to do. If that sounds weird, well... wait 'till you hear what's next. When I reached for "the cup," the "blood of Jesus," the BRIGHT purple grape juice... the cup EXPLODED! Now, I know what you are thinking, that I'm being a little dramatic and that it really didn't "explode." Well, ask my husband, Kevin!

He was right behind me. My face was covered! My neck, my pretty white outfit, it felt like I had splashed a lot more than that little cup on my face. We went back to our seats. Then Kevin said, "Let me see."

"I'm good," I said. "It's fine." I didn't want that to ruin my visit with Jesus, 'cause I was having one!

Later, when it was all over, I looked all over my face, my cute outfit. Guess what? Not even one spot. Not one! Purple grape juice... and still white? Yeah, right!

YES! I'm telling you! Not a spot! I was as white as snow! Covered. YES, COVERED by His blood! He was just reminding me. Oh how I love Him! And Oh, how He loves YOU!

<u>Psalm 91: 14-16 NIV</u>

Because he loves Me, says the Lord, I will rescue him; I will protect him, for he acknowledges My name. He will call on Me, and I will honor him; I will be with him in trouble, I will deliver him and honor him. With long life I will satisfy him and show him My salvation.

25

OUR PROMISE KEEPER

DO YOU KNOW who my God is? Let me tell you. He is the "Way Maker, Miracle Worker, Promise Keeper, the Light in the Darkness." *My God*—that is who He is! Just like the song "Way Maker" by Nigerian gospel singer Sinach says.

Jesus prayed...

> *"Father, I thank you*
> *that you have heard me."*
>
> John 11:41

That song was stuck in my head all day yesterday. I sang it. I thought it. I even yelled it! Because I have to believe it! Sometimes we have to encourage ourselves to believe what we already know to be true, because sometimes we forget. If we don't remind ourselves, we may believe the enemy's lies instead!

In His Word, He has promised us many things. However... WE have a part to play. We must BELIEVE that He wants us to TRUST Him, especially when things are the ugliest. Like when doubt tries to creep in and we may begin to think His promises might possibly NOT come to fruition. That's when we must trust and believe Him the most!

God, may our faith be like Your Faith! Thank you Father!

God is ALWAYS working! He goes before us and makes our crooked paths straight. Say this... "Father, today I choose to stand on YOUR promises. My personal promises! I choose to believe You and trust You! I look forward to what You are working on for me!"

Let me tell you something else... I AM BLESSED! HIGHLY FAVORED! AND BOLDLY LOVED! And if you receive Him and choose to believe... SO. ARE. YOU.

<u>Psalm 91: 1-2</u>

He who dwells in the shelter of the Most High
will abide in the shadow of the Almighty.

26

COUNT IT ALL JOY

DON'T MISTAKE OVULATION with an appendicitis. Don't miss it here... What I said was, *Don't mistake ovulation with an appendicitis!* WOOO! Now that's a nugget!

Out of everything we go through—every hardship, every bad situation, every not-so-good childhood, every bad break, every trial, every sickness, every breakup, every child who messes up... you get the picture. When we go through these things, sometimes it "feels" like the end of the world. Yeah... that's how the enemy wants you to "feel." Like it's an appendicitis.

However, when you're a child of the Most-High King, don't go by your "feelings." We must learn to stand on His promises! REJOICE! Like the birth of something new! Ovulation! Yeah... ovulation can be painful, don't get me wrong.

BUT... faith under pressure? Think about it like this...

Consider it a sheer gift, friends, when tests and challenges come at you from all sides. You know that under pressure, your faith-life is forced into the open and shows its true colors. So don't try to get out of anything prematurely. Let it do its work so you become mature and well-developed, not deficient in any way.

<u>James 1:2-4 MSG</u>

I'm writing this in the middle of the night. I'm awake because of ovulation. However, I am thankful for it. Not the pain it causes. Just like the things we go through in this life... I don't want to mistake ovulation as an appendicitis anymore!

Profiting from our Trials...

"... my brethren, count it all joy when you fall into various trials, knowing that the testing of your faith produces patience. But let patience have its perfect work, that you may be perfect and complete, lacking nothing."

<u>James 1:2-4</u>

The *Message Bible* calls it "Faith Under Pressure." *NKJV* calls it "Profiting from our Trials."

This is gold if you will hear it.

Have a great day!

<u>2 Corinthians 4:8-9</u>

We are hard pressed on every side, but not crushed; perplexed, but not in despair; persecuted, but not abandoned; struck down, but not destroyed.

{ 27 }

FAMILY TIME

AS I SIT here in one of my favorite restaurants that I frequent as much as possible, I can see and hear a daddy talking with his children. I can't hear every word he's saying, but I'm watching and listening to him interact with his kids. They are having what seems to be family time and they are talking about Jesus. He is teaching them what he believes and of course wants them to believe as well. He's asking them questions and they are answering. It's a beautiful thing. A moment in time for them to treasure. What a gift to be able to witness such a beautiful interaction.

Father's Day happens to be approaching as I'm writing this, which makes me think... Every father is teaching their children something. Whether they're spending time with them, or not. Whether he is talking with them about Jesus, or not. Whether they are present in the home, or not... children are learning from their fathers. Hey dads, and moms for that matter, what are we teaching our children?

Something to think about.

<u>Proverbs 20:7 NKJV</u>

The righteous man walks in his integrity;
His children are blessed after him.

28

LET THEM FLOW

THE OTHER DAY a friend of mine called me a "work horse" and I laughed out loud. However, that challenged me to ponder... I've never thought of myself as a "work horse." I have so many areas in my life that need to have more of a "work horse" mentality. But from that moment on, I wanted to see myself as a genuine "work horse." That's not being arrogant. That's just wanting to believe what His Word says to be true.

Think about it like this... I (We) can do all things through Christ who strengthens me (us) (Philippians 4:13). That's a promise I believe! I hope you believe that too! That is where our strength comes from. That's the way I survive.

A few years ago, on a particular Good Friday, something amazing happened at church. Through a series of events, leading up to that day, another friend of mine told me through tears that evening that "I took her breath away with my courage."

What? Me? Brave?

Well, after steeping on that one for a while, I decided that because of Him, I AM brave AND I am also strong and of a GOOD courage (Joshua 1:9). I believe part of being strong and of a good courage means just trusting in our Heavenly Father as our undeniably true source of strength.

Later that week, God gave me this, through my husband, Kevin:

<u>Exodus 14:13-14</u>

Do not be afraid! Stand still, and see the salvation of the Lord, which He will accomplish for you today. For the Egyptians (OUR PROBLEMS) whom you see today, you shall see again no more forever. The Lord will fight for you, and you shall hold your peace.

All we have to do is be still and know that He has us in the palm of His hand. Just like He always does... if we believe and trust.

I'm SO thankful for my friends, and especially my hubby who took the time to speak LIFE into me. Without them really knowing, except for Kevin, each one of them, through their words, helped me in several situations that just happened to be going on in my life at the time.

So today, if you think about someone positively, tell them! They may just need a nugget from God, spoken through you, to help them with situations you know nothing about. Be a vessel for Him. He wants us to be.

Something to think about.

John 7:38 NIV

Whoever believes in Me, as Scripture has said, rivers of living water will flow from within them.

29

PRAYER CHANGES THINGS

DID YOU KNOW God hears our prayers? God not only hears our prayers but He acts on our prayers. All prayer is, is a conversation with Him, just like talking with a friend. We may think He's not even listening but know this... He hears all and knows all things. He's always working. Always in motion behind the scenes of the stories of our lives. I love it when He answers our prayers in a completely different way than we could have EVER imagined. Sometimes He just makes me laugh out loud. Thank you, Father!

I believe when we "cast all our cares" on Him, He acts on our concerns as prayers even when we don't know how to express them. He already knows every little detail. He KNOWS what we care about. He knows everything and guess what?! He genuinely CARES about what concerns we have. Even the little things that we wouldn't even think to tell Him. Talk to Him about them anyway! Tell Him first.

Most people in our lives don't want to hear all the details. My husband, for example. He would rather me tell him the guts of my concerns and leave out ALL the little details when possible. Not our Father. He loves when we tell Him everything, or nothing at all. I'm so thankful that we can tell Him anything OR just sit quietly with Him. Trust me when I say, He knows and understands our hearts especially when we can't seem to find the words to tell Him.

Believe that He answers your prayers. Believe that He hears us. Believe that He loves you SO much. Have a great day!

"Something happens when you pray, that doesn't happen when you don't pray. So who is missing out today if you choose not to pray?"

—Dick Eastman

Luke 12 6-7 TPT

What is the value of your soul to God? Could your worth be defined by any amount of money? God doesn't abandon or forget even the small sparrow he has made. How could He forget or abandon you?

30

I AM AN EAGLE

NO MATTER WHAT'S going on in your world... No matter what's going on with the ones you love... No matter what situation you may be facing, or the season you or your loved ones are walking through... Remember this: If they still have breath, there is STILL hope. Even if they DON'T have breath, there can still be HOPE!

However, when we take our eyes off our Savior and His Word and His Promises and we look at our situation and how bad we think it is... that's when we allow fear in. And fear? Fear is not from God. Fear is from the enemy. And fear... is a liar!

I love all these different translations of Psalms 94:19:

- In the multitude of my anxieties within me, Your comforts delight my soul! (NKJV)
- When the cares of my heart are many, Your consolations cheer my soul. (ESV)
- When doubts filled my mind, Your comfort gave me renewed hope and cheer. (NLT)
- When I was upset and beside myself, You calmed me down and cheered me up. (MSG)
- Whenever my busy thoughts were out of control, the soothing comfort of Your presence calmed me down and overwhelmed me with delight. (TPT)

TODAY... Stand on this promise from your Father:

But they that wait upon the Lord shall renew their strength; they shall mount up with the wings as eagles; they shall run, and not be weary; and they shall walk, and not faint.

Isaiah 40:31 KJV

HOPE has a name... His name is JESUS and today I am an EAGLE! That's my choice. What's yours? Have a great day!

Hebrews 3:13 NIV

But encourage one another daily, as long as
it is called "Today," so that none of you may
be hardened by sin's deceitfulness.

31

HE IS OUR HOPE

Romans 15:13 NKJV

Now may the God of Hope fill you with all joy and peace in believing, that you may abound in Hope by the power of the Holy Spirit.

Romans 15:13 TPT

Now may God the inspiration and foundation of hope, fill you to overflowing with uncontainable joy in perfect peace as you trust in Him. And may the power of the Holy Spirit continually surround your life with his super-abundance until you radiate with hope!

It's hard NOT to get excited! As we TRUST in Him.

TRUST HIM! Trust Him with your everything! He loves you SO much! He may love me the most! I am His favorite you know? But SO ARE YOU! You need to KNOW that!

Hold on to that concept today! We ARE His favorites! Blessings!

Isaiah 62:3

You shall also be a crown of glory in the hand of the LORD, And a royal diadem in the hand of your God.

32

GOD IS OUR STRATEGY

WHAT IF WE knew we were going into battle but were not prepared? What if we went to war without any weapons or tactical experience or knowledge of the enemy we were in front of? Today I celebrate victory! Victory for battles we have fought and possibly the ones that may be in our future. We have already won! Today I celebrate Christ. Victory was ours for the taking even before the fight was fought. Because of Him. Because He chose the cross. Because He loved us first!

Several years ago my husband and I, several of our closest family members, and some amazing friends God brought into our lives for such a time as this, well... we went to battle. We learned how to go to war. Battle after battle we continued forward. One. Day. At. A. Time.

Sometimes, it looked like we were losing. But we never lost hope! No matter WHAT it looked like! We stood on MANY of God's promises. And we BELIEVED them. All of them!

Today I can say, I wouldn't change a thing about the journey BECAUSE of the closeness and intimacy that we may not have known with our Heavenly Father, had we not experienced the things He allowed us to walk through. And for that... I am extremely thankful!

One thing is for sure... We don't want to waste our pain. Not one bit! There are things we have learned through it all, that we believe could benefit others. Strategic battle plans and warfare methods that got us through to victory! Praise God! FOREVER STARTS TODAY! For that... and for our friends who stood and still stand by our side and so much more... I am forever grateful! Thank you!

Thank You Father! TETELESTAI! Thank you Jesus!

<u>Hebrews 6:18</u>

So God has given both His promise and His oath. These two things are unchangeable because it is impossible for God to lie. Therefore, we who have fled to Him for refuge can have great confidence as we hold to the hope that lies before us.

33

HAPPINESS IS AN INSIDE JOB

OFTEN IN OUR lives, we look to others to fill a void in our heart that is not theirs to fill. The void was purposely put there by our Creator for Him to fill and Him to fill alone. Ever since I was a little girl, on up until I had my own children, I wanted so badly for my dad to fill that void. It was almost an obsession. I wanted his approval. An "atta girl." His time. His blessing. Bottom line, I wanted his love. Don't get me wrong, I know my dad did love me. But it was not possible for him to fill that void.

Many times throughout our marriage, I've looked to my husband, Kevin, to fill a similar void. To "make me happy." To give me what I think I want and think I need. Thank goodness, I made a discovery! That void or emptiness was not theirs to fill. It never was!

God purposely put a yearning inside of each of us that NO human or thing can fill but HIM. A God-shaped hole or a vacuum. A round hole that we keep trying to shove something square in that will never fit! When I figured that out, life became so much sweeter. It took a lot of pressure off of the ones I love. It was never their place to make me happy! God desires us to desire Him! He wants to be our number one! Happiness is an inside job. Hear me.

If you can grasp this, it will change your life forever! Your relationships. Your happiness. Think about it like this… God wants us, His creation, to want Him. He wants us to spend time getting to know Him. He's actually jealous when we don't! I think that's so cool. The Creator of the universe, of ALL the universes, our Father, wants to spend time with you and me. That is wonderful enough, but that He actually desires it, that it gives Him satisfaction and joy and pleasure, is almost too much for my understanding.

In turn, when we spend time with Him, it also fills that desire IN US that ONLY He can satisfy. Thank you Father! It's a WIN-WIN! … WHEN we fill that void with Him! This not only changes our lives, it has the potential to change the ones around us! Oh how He loves us!

"There is a God-shaped vacuum in the heart of each man, which cannot be satisfied by any created thing but God the Creator, made known through Jesus Christ."

—Blaise Pascal

<u>Psalm 37:4 ESV</u>

Delight yourself in the Lord, and He will
give you the desires of your heart.

34

BE STILL AND KNOW

THE PAIN THAT you've been feeling, can't compare to the joy that's coming (Romans 8:18). I have so many friends who are hurting right now. Maybe you do as well. One thing or another in their lives is amiss. So many that have asked for prayers. So many that are sick and/or full of despair. Many who have loved ones who are, well, pretty dang distant. Some who are sad, mad, or confused.

My heart is heavy for so many. Anyway, maybe you are heavy too? Why don't we just sit right here for a sec... and just let Him hold us? Maybe His hug is just what we need? Lean in and breathe deeply. Feel His breath as well. Listen for His heartbeat. Don't forget how loved you are. God is great and so very kind. He is ever so precious and very present so let's just steep in His love for a minute, okay? He wants you to know He hasn't forgotten you.

"Come closer to Me. Live close to My heart, my child. I will bring you into the secret place and give you rest. Let nothing trouble you. The enemy is a defeated foe. My presence will be your peace.

"Lay your head upon My shoulder and rest with Me. Entwine your heart with Mine until we are one. It is the slanderer who will always wound you in your weakness. But I will strengthen you until you stand complete, wearing My robe and my armor."[5]

Whisper His name... *Jesus.* Or maybe even scream it. Whatever you need. He's always listening.

---

[5] —passionandfireministries on Instagram.
https://www.instagram.com/p/CU4skXfr73X/

<u>2 Corinthians 1:3-4</u>

Praise be to the God and Father of our Lord Jesus Christ, the Father of compassion and the God of all comfort, who comforts us in all our troubles, so that we can comfort those in any trouble with the comfort we ourselves receive from God.

35

GRACE

YEARS AGO I heard some lies about someone very close to me. The lies actually made me laugh out loud for a just a second. Then I got SO stinkin' mad! Deep in my gut, it hurt me terribly. Immediately I wanted to confront (punch) these "so-called lifelong friends" and "set them straight." But I didn't. I've done that in other situations and it just causes more chaos. It adds fuel to the fire. It makes what you're stirring in stink even more.

I love these people. And I love the one they're lying about. I consider them all my family/friends, not my enemies. However, God's word says...

"If your enemy is hungry, feed him. If he is thirsty, give him a drink. For in doing so

you will heap coals of fire (shame and regret) on his head."

Romans 12:20

I have also tried this. Although it's hard at first and not something that comes natural. However, the more you do it, the easier it gets. With God's help, of course. It's part of learning to trust Him. And trust me, the results are amazing.

Because God's Word also says...

We do not wrestle against flesh and blood, (people), but against principalities, against powers, against the rulers of the darkness of this age, against spiritual hosts of wickedness in the heavenly places.

Ephesians 6:12

The enemy is spreading these lies, not the people I love... because they don't realize they're being used as his tools. But they are. He uses who will let him. Ouch.

My prayer for us all is that we would hear from Heaven. I don't have to defend the one they're lying about. I just have to be still... and know that

He is God. Trust Him. And love. Whew. Still a hard one. But His grace and mercies are new EVERY day. Not only for me, but for EVERYONE! So thankful.

Through the Lord's mercies we are not consumed, Because His compassions fail not. They are new every morning; Great is Your faithfulness.

36

CRY OUT TO HIM

AND WHEN HE (a blind beggar named Bartimaeus) heard that it was Jesus, he began to cry out and say, "Jesus, Son of David, have mercy on me!" Then many warned him to be quiet; but he cried out all the more, "Son of David, have mercy on me!"

Then Jesus stood still and commanded him to be called.

Then they called the blind man, saying to him, "Be of good cheer. Rise, He is calling you."

Mark 10:47-49 NKJV

WHEN IT COMES to crying out to the Savior, don't let anyone tell you to be quiet. Don't let anyone try to shush you. You cry out to Jesus! He WILL stand still for you. He hears you! He loves you! Call out to Him today. Have Faith! Believe! Live with expectancy! And be thankful that He hears you.

Have a great day.

I waited patiently for the Lord; He turned to me and heard my cry.

37

THANKFUL

WHEN YOU WALK through a storm, all the way through, then you turn around and look back and the storm has dissipated and all you see is a rainbow... or sunshine... or the hope of what was prayed for... what you fought every battle for... what you trusted God for standing there healthy and whole... Well, all you can do is praise Him for His goodness and His mercy. And you are thankful. And words can't describe the happiness He has put in your heart for the things you have learned.

When you know you wouldn't trade a second for every raindrop. Every lightning strike. Every sound of thunder. Every sleepless night. Every tear that was shed.

Today, I praise my Father for fruition. For His completion. His VICTORY. TETELESTAI. It is finished. *Thank you Father.*

If you can't say this yourself, or if you are still in a storm... Hold tight to His promises! And don't let go. Let Him and He will. Trust Him. Know His promises. And believe what He says about your situation. If you don't know what He says, talk with your Father. He wants you to.

With a grateful heart, prayers and blessings.

<u>Isaiah 43:2 NKJV</u>

When you go through deep waters, I will be
with you. When you go through rivers of
difficulty, you will
not drown.

38

NO FEAR IS FROM YOUR FATHER

HERE'S A NUGGET...

God has NOT given us the spirit of fear, but of POWER, and of LOVE, and of a SOUND mind.

<u>2 Timothy 1:7</u>

Did you get that? Please hear this! When we live in fear, the devil has a stronghold on our lives... on our minds! Any fear we let into our thoughts, our heads, our hearts, our souls, here it is... IS NOT FROM GOD!

When we worry, that's a form of fear. Worry is a tactic of the enemy. When we know this ahead of time, we can counteract that lie with 2 Timothy 1:7, which is a promise from your Father. A gift that He has given you. IF you will open and receive it, THEN it is yours to believe. A promise to stand on.

Remember this, fear is a liar! Open His gifts today. Receive His promises and have a freedom in Christ like never before!

Have a wonderful fear free life!

John 14:27 NIV

Peace I leave with you; My peace I give you. I do not give to you as the world gives. Do not let your hearts be troubled and do not be afraid.

39

FORGIVENESS

I THINK THE hardest person I ever had to forgive... was myself. Actually, for sure. It is me. On a daily basis. We mess up. We shouldn't. However, we do. At least I do, anyway.

"Forgiveness."

It's almost therapeutic just to say it out loud. Go ahead. Say it out loud... "FORGIVENESS."

Now say this... "I forgive you," or "I forgive _____ (their name here)," or "I forgive you, Michelle," or "_____, (your name here), I forgive you."

If we can't even say it privately out loud to ourselves, how can we practice saying it out loud to others? Or even privately towards others, in our hearts? Genuinely, from our hearts?

We have to receive our own forgiveness. Others may not ever receive our forgiveness. But that's okay... they may in time. We can pray for that. But our job is to forgive them, anyway. To forgive others as well as ourselves.

If you're having trouble forgiving people in your life who have wronged you or ones you love, or wronged people you don't even know... ask your Father in Heaven to help you. Jesus died on the cross for our forgiveness. If we can't forgive others, why would God forgive us? He paid the price... we didn't.

Have a great day in Him!

<u>Psalms 103:10-12 TPT</u>

You may discipline us for our many sins, but never as much as we really deserve. Nor do You get even with us for what we've done. Higher than the highest heavens—that's how high Your tender mercy extends! Greater than the grandeur of heaven above is the greatness of Your loyal love, towering over all who fear You and bow down before You! Farther than from a sunrise to a sunset—that's how far You've removed our guilt from us.

40

THE TRUEST SACRIFICE

I JUST THOUGHT of something... I would NEVER give my son or daughter for ANY of you! I'm sorry, but I wouldn't. I just couldn't... I don't think so, anyway. However, God did just that!

He would have given HIS son for just one of us! Thankful our Father gave His son, Jesus, for us ALL!

For God so loved the world that He gave His ONLY Son, that whoever believes in Him should not perish but have everlasting life. For God did not send His Son into the world to condemn the world, but that the world through Him might be saved.

<u>John 3:16-17</u>

He loves us THAT much! Salvation... the greatest gift ever given. Have you opened yours yet? It's available for everyone! What an amazing present given to us freely that cost so very much. All we have to do is just believe!

Thank you Jesus!

Have a wonderful day!

<u>1 John 4:19 NKJV</u>

We love Him because He first loved us.

41

THE RIGHT ROCK

IT BREAKS MY heart when I hear people say, "Well... they're just gonna have to hit rock bottom before they'll ever change." Or, "Maybe if they go to prison, they'll come out different."

What if we loved people SO HARD they didn't have to hit rock bottom? What if we went to war for the ones who can't or won't, who just don't have the strength to do it for themselves? What if we fought for our marriages instead of just throwing in the towel because the grass looks greener on the other side? What if we got up EVERY morning to pray for someone in a crisis? Or loved a paralyzed friend so much we carried him to town on his bed, climbed to the top of a building, cut a hole in a concrete-type roof and lowered him down, thinking that if we could just get him in the room with Jesus, he would be healed?

Now that's going to war! What if we stayed up all night to pray? Or went without a meal or two or for days even to fast and pray for someone you don't even know that well? What if you did that for your own child? Or a complete stranger?

Don't give up! Don't give up on people. Don't throw your hands in the air and say things like rock bottom. Unless you throw your hands up to Heaven! And help them find the REAL Rock instead! His name is Jesus!

Go to WAR for them! Ask God to show you your unique strategy for whatever the situation. Fight! Fight like you would want someone to fight for you.

<u>John 15:13 NKJV</u>

Greater love has no one than this, than to lay down one's life for his friends.

42

INSIDE OUT

AS I LOOK in the mirror these days... I see something new. Something I've not seen before. Me... Me different. And I like her. I guess what I'm trying to say is I like who I'm becoming. A more mature me... Yes, an older version of who I am, and I think I like it.

Sure, there are plenty of things I might would change about myself, but in general, I like who I am in Christ. Apart from Him, well... I'm pretty dang ugly.

I'm His favorite, ya know? I just love that! You're his favorite too! However, you have to choose to believe it. First you need to know what your Father says about you. If you don't know, then go know. Start by reading His Word. Sit with Him. Ask Him to show you. Google what your Heavenly Father says about you.

God says... *I knew you before I formed you in your mother's womb.* He says you are a child of the Most-High King! Your Daddy owns the cattle on a thousand hills! He even owns all the hills! You are the apple of His eye! He knows every hair on your head! He knows every tear you have shed. He knows your thoughts before you think them!

I recommend you believe that you are His favorite every day... for the rest of your life. It'll change *who you are* from the inside out. So very thankful He loved me first. Guess what? He loved you first, too! Believe it! Allow yourself to be loved today!

<u>2 Corinthians 3:18 NKJV</u>

But we all, with unveiled face, beholding as
in a mirror the glory of the Lord, are being
transformed into the same image from glory
to glory, just as by the Spirit of the Lord.

43

LEARNING TO LISTEN

A FRIEND ONCE said to me, "Learning to hear the voice of the Holy Spirit is kind of like playing a game." How fun. I wanna play! So I did. I began asking God about certain things and then slowing my mind and trying to hear Him. Just like most games, the more you play, the easier they get.

For example, "Okay God, you know I have misplaced my checkbook. You also know where it is. Could you please tell me? I need it to pay bills. Thank you, Father."

And then, get quiet, and listen. I was amazed at how much fun this could actually be. SO very thankful for my dear friend Janey for teaching me so many things over the years. However, this may be my favorite!

A few days later, I read a verse in my Bible...

Romans 15:13 NKJV

Now may the God of Hope fill you with all joy and peace in believing, that you may abound in Hope by the power of the Holy Spirit.

Beside it was a date and another friend's name who sent this particular verse to me via text. She also sent, "I don't know why but I think I'm supposed to send this to you." So she had heard, and she listened, then she sent me that verse.

Four years later, I thought I would let her know what happened when I received it back then. First, I sent her a text asking if she remembered sending it to me. She said yes. I sent her another text explaining what transpired after she obeyed our Holy Spirit's gentle nudge. I wrote to her:

"I was at church. We weren't even having a regular service. I just needed to go worship. Our youth was having a service, so we went. I was trying my best to quiet my mind and just be with Jesus. However, my

137

mom kept calling my phone. When I finally answered, she was hysterically upset, crying out for help. Peace... I could not give her. Nothing I would say calmed her. This was our normal at this stage. My mom was suffering from dementia."

My friend texted me at that moment and I texted the verse she sent me to my precious mother. It immediately calmed her. Then I was able to worship. I needed to, and God knew it. God used my friend to calm my mom so I could draw from Him.

Kind of funny, I think. He is so good. He knows what we need. And He uses who will let Him. We have no idea why sometimes. Thank you sweet Robin for being obedient and oh so precious.

The lesson here is this... Learn to hear the Holy Spirit. And when you hear Him, listen to what He says. And when you listen to His voice, the next step is to DO what He says. He won't ask you to do ANYTHING He won't equip you to do.

My friend had NO idea why she was supposed to send me that verse. And sometimes we never know why God asks us to do certain things. That doesn't matter. Our job is to just obey His voice. He may tell you later. He may not. I believe we will know in Heaven. Either way, Ask, Hear, Listen and

Obey. And if He blesses you, like He did me, let that person know.

It will bless them too!

Isaiah 30:21 ESV

And your ears shall hear a word behind you, saying, "This is the way, walk in it," when you turn to the right or when you turn to the left.

44

THANK HIM ANYWAY

GRATITUDE IS AN attitude. However, it's also a choice that we forget to choose, at times. Or at least I do.

They say, "Things happen in threes," whoever "they" are. The day that Pete, one of our steers, died, before we even buried him we found one of our momma cows killed by coyotes while she was calving.

Earlier that morning, we drove four hours one-way to look at a much-needed truck for work. It wouldn't even crank, although it cranked WONDERFULLY the day before (insert eye roll emoji) and was not ANYTHING like the pictures we had seen or what the seller had tried to sell us over the phone. We were home by 1:00 p.m. with no truck, and yes, I was tired. I was already mentally and physically tired from the week before. Then there was Pete. And now a momma cow AND her baby.

Kevin fed hay first as I saddled and rode one of our horses around checking cows and fences in hopes that nothing else would be found wrong for that day. Well, the pump had stopped working. So we carried water for horses. And after burying the three of them (Pete, momma cow and baby), Kevin worked about two hours that day and three hours the next, just on the pump until it was fixed.

We were supposed to go to a roping the following weekend. However, a small motor on our horse trailer (my cabin on wheels) was not working among a few other things that were being ornery, so our trip was canceled, and I was disappointed, to say the least... And that was another set of three problems!

The Pete situation was hard, yet I found in me some things I hadn't seen in a while. With the help of my lifelong friend, Dianne, I was able to give that steer as many shots as I had to without hyperventilating or passing out. (Needles are not my thing.) God gave me strength!

We needed to know just how bad of a coyote problem we had, and it was bad. I have a guy, however, who took care of that, thankfully.

The trailer had some issues that we found at home and not on the road, or in 4-degree weather. And the pump went out when we were home and had time to work on it, not during the week when we needed to be working at other stuff. Like jobs. Or while we were gone to a roping and our daughter and her husband, Derek, would have been stuck carrying water for horses.

So I'm thankful! And if I sound like I'm complaining, I'm not. We are so blessed and I'm grateful for ALL our life lessons, whether they are fun or extremely hard. The hard stuff's where we learn. And where we learn to trust. To trust Him.

Something to think about.

<u>1 Thes 5:16-18 TPT</u>

Let joy be your continual feast. Make your life a prayer. And in the midst of everything be always giving thanks, for this is God's perfect plan for you in Christ Jesus.

45

PIGGYBACK RIDE

I WAS STEEPING in this precious verse when this picture (at the end of this chapter) popped up on my phone. This is my husband, Kevin, carrying our granddaughter, Raylee Jade.

The beloved of the Lord shall dwell in safety by Him, who shelters him all the day long; and he shall dwell between His shoulders.

<u>Deuteronomy 33:12</u>

Isn't that wonderful? Just think about it. Our Father wants us to dwell with Him! To give us shelter. His shelter. And when we do... we are safe in His care. He goes before us. He makes our crooked paths straight! All while carrying us when we trust Him.

I think I'll take a piggyback ride today (and every day) with my Heavenly Father. He shelters us between His shoulders! No matter what's going on in your life right now, I encourage you to take a piggyback ride as well! He sure does want you to!

He loves us SO much!

Have a great day!

<u>Psalm 91:4 MSG</u>

His huge outstretched arms protect you –
under them you're perfectly safe; His arms
fend off all harm.

46

YOU MATTER

NOT TOO LONG ago I jotted down some thoughts that came to mind for a sweet friend who needed a little pick-me-up. Maybe some of us could use a word or two from this for ourselves. Read it once, or over and over until they begin to sink in. I sent her this...

YOU MATTER! You really do matter. You are important. Just because you didn't go to college doesn't mean you can't. And just because you did, does not make you who you are. You are a child of The Most-High King. That's what makes you beautiful.

Be confident in who you are. Be confident in Who's you are. Be confident in where you are. Be confident in where you're going. Be thankful for the way things are. Be thankful for the way things can be.

If you don't like your current situation, change it. Be thankful for small beginnings. Consistently constant. CONSISTENTLY CONSTANT! Do everything as if you were doing it for the Lord. EVERYTHING! Laundry, cooking, cleaning, LIFE! Do LIFE as if you were doing it for your Father.

Take care of yourself. And don't feel guilty about it. Spend time with Him. Just you and Him. Every day. Pray. Exercise. Eat right. Every day is a new day. If you messed up today, start over. Now. You can do ANYTHING! Say this: "I can do ALL things through Christ who strengthens me! All day! Everyday!"

Keep on keeping on! The more you do, the more you will be able to do. The less you do, the less you will be able to do. SO DO MORE! Have a BLESSED day! This is your BEST day! Make it count! And then do it again tomorrow! BLESSINGS! And remember this... The Best Is Yet To Come!

Love you,

Michelle

<u>Colossians 3:17 NKJV</u>

And whatever you do in word or deed, do all
in the name of the Lord Jesus, giving thanks
to God the Father through Him.

47

HE KNOWS MY NAME

HE WAITS FOR me. He listens. He watches for me to look at Him. He loves when I run to Him. And when I'm still. When I listen for His whisper. He whispers because He's so close and always has been. He holds me tight. Ever so gently. He gives me His strength. He calls my name. And I hear Him... I will never be the same.

<u>Exodus 33;17 NKJV</u>

So the Lord said to Moses, "I will also do this thing that you have spoken; for you have found grace in My sight, and I know you by name."

48

TO MY YOUNGER SELF

A FRIEND ASKED me a question... and I thought about it. If I could go back and tell my younger self some things, I would want her to know this:

You. Are. Loved. Don't look for what you think you want. Ask God what is best for you. God knows the end before the beginning. Put Him first. Period. It always works out. Always. If you want to know His plan for your life... love Him. Know Him. Trust Him with your everything! TRUST HIM. Talk to Him about every detail. He loves you unconditionally. Always has. Always will. READ His word. And hide it in your heart. You will need it there someday. You are beautiful even though you sometimes think you're not. Let beauty come from within. Be consistently constant. In everything you do. Take one day at a time. Laugh. Everyday! Live in the moment. And plan well. However, don't worry about tomorrow. You are a survivor. Always remember... He will never leave you nor forsake you!

Deuteronomy 31:6

Be strong and of good courage, do not fear nor be afraid of them; for the Lord your God, He is the One who goes with you. He will not leave you nor forsake you.

49

MORNING BEAUTY

DO YOU EVER just wake up happy? We should... every day of our lives. "Oh sure," you say. "You have NO idea what I'm going through." Doesn't matter. Jesus said as long as you live in the world, you were going to have trouble. But you're not just in the world. You're *in Jesus* in the world, and that makes all the difference. You're in Him and He's overcome every kind of trouble there is.

I have told you these things, so that in Me you have (perfect) peace and confidence. In the world you have tribulations and trials and distress and frustration but be of good cheer... I have overcome the world.

John 16:33

This morning I was thinking about several things our family has walked through. Big or small to us, they all matter to our Daddy. He has shown me that He cares about every little detail of our lives.

For instance, when you misplace your checkbook. I asked Holy Spirit where it was... I then stopped to listen and He told me. Or, when you fall and watch as all the Christmas presents you're carrying break and glass flies all around you but then when you go to clean out the box of broken glass... NOTHING is broken. Or, when your husband buries his cellphone on a huge job site, and he asked God to show him where it is and He tells him exactly where to dig and guess what? There it is!

I could go on and on but I just want you to hear what I'm trying to say... Trust Him. Know Him. Listen.

Listen... Here's the key: Do you know Him? Get to know Him if you don't. Spend time with Him. Ask Him to show Himself to you in the little things. Then, when something big happens—and it will—you can lean on Him and walk it out with Joy and Peace. If you know Him, you are an overcomer, too!

Blessings!

<u>Isaiah 41:13 NIV</u>

For I am the Lord your God who takes hold of your right hand, do not fear... I will help you.

50

FEAR NOT

THE ENEMY TRIES to trick us, you know. I think fear might be his favorite tool. It only becomes a weapon when we let it develop, when we let it in. He doesn't know our thoughts. He studies our mannerisms. Then he shoots. He shoots us with his pesky little arrows. The ones that he knows will get us into doubt. If we are suited for battle, those arrows just bounce off. BUT if we aren't wearing our armor... then one may find a weak spot to penetrate... Eventually. Then another... Then another... Those fiery darts can grow our fear into a monstrosity... If we let them.

It starts with only a thought. Then we begin to dwell on it. It grows, and before long we are consumed. We have to teach ourselves not to do that! It doesn't come natural. But it can if we decide and develop the right mechanisms. Stop those thoughts. You and I ain't got time for that mess!

On a recent road trip, Kevin started talking about fear. And I typed as he talked. I tweaked it a little but I think he had a revelation of where fear comes from. *Thank you, Father for the wisdom that you have available when we seek You!* Maybe someone needs to hear this as well. So here it is:

Fear is not mine. Fear that we've been given is the enemy's fear. Hear this. God has NOT given us the spirit of fear. The enemy has given us his fear. It's not ours! When we have fear, it's him trying to be free of fear by giving it to us. God told Joshua no man shall stand up before you. The fear is not yours. Fear is the enemy's. The enemy is afraid of us!

Not that he's afraid of say… Kevin… or Michelle… or you. But that God said "Kevin is my creation. I have created Kevin. And that is good! Do not let him steal and destroy what I have told you! Not for one second! Don't let him (the enemy) steal what I have promised you."

Be strong and of good courage. *Rak Chazak Amats[6]! Be STRONG and of GOOD COURAGE.* Let

---

[6] "Rak Chazak Amats! All Strength and Courage for the Glory of Our God! "Rak Chazak Amats" is an ancient Hebrew war cry that

that be your war-cry! God has NO fear! Fear is not one of His descriptions. Fear is not from God! Fear is a false reality. Why do we pray and ask God for something and at the same time we are fearful? Wouldn't that just cancel out our prayer?

Oh yes! I believe God can do ANYTHING HE WANTS! But our *faith* is our power. Without faith... well... it is impossible to please God. You first must believe that He *is*, and that He is a rewarder to those who diligently seek Him. Seek Him!

Faith cancels out our fear. We've all been given the same amount of faith. It's how we use it or exercise it... that will determine how it grows!

Pray this: "Father... let my faith be like Yours."

Christians can adopt." —https://bibleinspirations.org/rak-chazak-amats-all-strength-and-courage-for-the-glory-of-our-god/

<u>Psalm 56:3 NKJV</u>

Whenever I am afraid,
I will trust in You.

ACKNOWLEDGEMENTS

THERE ARE SO many wonderful people who have encouraged me to pursue this journey... that I could never name you all or thank you enough! To every one of you... I am forever grateful! Without each of you, I don't think I would have ever thought that anyone would have wanted to read my "thinking out loud" in book form.

To my Heavenly Father, I pray You are glorified by the words on these pages and that someone reading this book will trust You with their EVERYTHING! That Jesus will speak to them and that they will know He loves them like I know You love me.

To my husband, Kevin. Watching you and standing by you through this life has taught me how to push through very hard things. The dedication and sacrifices... the discipline and fortitude that you have displayed from such a very young age... the ability you have to OUTLAST no matter what... has been nothing but beautiful to me. To watch you father and fight for our children is such a gift. I thank you for being by my side and allowing me the space to be me. Being a spiritual leader and teaching our family has been the greatest gift you could ever have given us! Thank you for loving God first. This book is dedicated to you. I thank God that He made you exactly like you are... perfect for me. Thank you for *so* much inspiration and insight on life. This could not have happened without you. I love you.

To my children, Jessica and Michael. To my grandchildren, Raylee and Evelyn. To my sweet momma and my precious Aunt Mimi. You have all touched my life immensely. I love you all!

To Kayla... you are a Godsend! I could not have done this without you! Thank you for everything!

To my friend Gary... the encourager! Your cookies are in the oven! Thank you for believing in me!

Thank you ALL who believed in me. I am forever grateful!

ABOUT THE AUTHOR

SOME HAVE CALLED her a Hope Dealer. Others have considered her the Dog Lady. However, if you ask Michelle Hargus, she would tell you she is a child of The Most High King. Her most favorite compliment ever was, "You have the ability to make people feel comfortable."

Michelle adores her family. She is a retired professional pet stylist of over 30 years. She enjoys being "Emmie" to her grandkids, riding horses, team roping, and genuinely making people laugh out loud. Her husband, Kevin, is her favorite. She loves life and Jesus and wants everyone to know how much He loves them. She lives in rural North Carolina where she enjoys being in nature and eating really good food.